PRAISE FOR CHRISTOPH PAUL

"Brave in its playfulness, *A Confederacy of Hot Dogs* brings Bukowski to Bizarro for the Facebook generation. As with the best satire, Christoph Paul's hilarious no-holds-barred novella has a lot of love for what it mocks. The most genuinely fun book I've read in many years."

— **Alexander Boldizar, author of *The Ugly***

"Christoph Paul might be our generation's patron saint of crass. Charming, funny, and perverse, *A Confederacy of Hot Dogs* will have you pissing yourself and feeling warm fuzzies in equal measure. Read it, and set it down, and whisper to yourself, "I love you, YOU FUCK.""

— **Brian Allen Carr, author of *Sip* and *Mother Fucking Sharks***

"A hilarious and transgressive love letter to *A Confederacy of Dunces* and struggling artists in the digital age."

— **Jayme Karales, author of *Disorderly* and creator of *LowRes Wunderbred***

A CONFEDERACY OF HOT DOGS

CHRISTOPH PAUL

This novel is dedicated to the memory of my mother. She taught me to laugh at the fucked things in life. I miss and love you mom.

Where the fuck do all these people get their confidence? I've seen their work and they should probably kill themselves.

— Philip LoPresti

PART 1

1

Philip LoPresti sat on his nacho cheese stained couch with his laptop opened to Facebook while *Dracula 3D* played on his wide screen TV. It was certainly not Argento's best work, but LoPresti enjoyed the cool kills and the eerie atmosphere. He didn't care if the dialogue was garbage or the story made no sense.

Phil was a huge horror fan and owned a massive collection of DVDs and Blu-rays, but because of his recent firing at a t-shirt store located on the Jersey Shore he couldn't afford to buy Argento's new Film, *My Daughter Is Diabolically Hot,* starring Asia Argento.

He heard the Facebook notification ping and noticed that a fellow author he hated had posted that their new novella *The Premature Penis Ejaculators vs. The Alien Vaginas from Pluto Part 3* was live on Kindle. It quickly got 42 Likes and rose to the top of his Facebook feed.

WHAT IS THIS NONSENSE! LoPresti thought.

He had recently put out his new poetry collection *I'd Drown in Your Vaginal Blood: 20 Love Sonnets* for his one and only true love, Missy, his girlfriend and muse, but that link only received 12 likes.

Missy wasn't home and wouldn't be back from work for another hour. Phil hadn't worked in a month and neither his books nor his photography were selling anywhere near enough to help pay the rent. Out of desperation for cash, Phil had entered a Photography-art show in Montclair, New Jersey that offered a prize of $500 dollars.

Unemployment had ended a week ago for Phil and he needed money to pay for groceries, and more importantly, to get Missy to stop bitching at him.

Phil had not been fired for incompetency. No, he lost his job for insubordination and horror snobbery.

His old boss at the t-shirt shop had brought in 50 shirts of the cult favorite horror film *Nightbreed*. While Phil was a huge Clive Barker fan, there was only one film that was forever banned from his vast collection, and that film was *Nightbreed*. Phil found the movie very disappointing. He didn't care that it was a metaphor for gay sex or that it had rabid fans. It was the worst film he had ever seen, and it brought him existential despair that even a genius like Clive Barker could make such shitty art.

"You're a horror guy, LoPresti," said his boss the day he brought in the shirts. "I think the *Nightbreed* shirt looks cool and will sell well to all the Goth kids. You'd wear it, right?"

"I think you should sell it," Phil shot back. "But only to people who will wipe their asses with it. FUCK *NIGHTBREED*!"

"What? What the hell, I bought 50 of these shirts. They look cool. They will be front and center in the horror section."

"I will only sell this as toilet paper," said Phil, taking a shirt out of the package and placing it in the gag toilet paper section that included Kim Kardashian Ass Wipes and poop colored Charmin rolls.

"Get that away from the toilet paper, Phil! These shirts weren't cheap. I bought them from the Armenians!"

"You bought them from assholes! This shirt, like the movie,

should be banned or shoved up Clive Barker's asshole! I'm still disappointed by that abortion of a film."

"I thought you liked horror stuff. Jesus kid, I'm getting tired of your bullshit."

Phil's face turned red with anger. "If you told Jesus that dying for our sins included Clive Barker making *Nightbreed* he'd get his ass off that fucking cross."

"You know what, LoPresti, you are a good-looking skinny guinea and these stupid young broads like ya, hell some of these depressed Goth girls would probably buy horseshit from you, but I've had it up to here were with this *bafangool* I'm-too-cool-for-school-bullshit. You act like this every fucking day and I'm sick of it."

"Well, every fucking day I feel disenchantment that Clive Barker made such a horrible film."

"Ok Mr. hot-shot-poet-I'm-too-fucking-good-for-*Nightbreed*, you're gonna agree to sell these shirts or else you're ..." the boss stopped talking as a young teenage poser-punk kid walked into the store.

Phil grabbed the shirt and said, "Hey kid, have you heard about the next big thing, using shitty horror film t-shirts to wipe your asshole. Fall Out Boy is already writing a song about how cool it is."

"I love Fall Out Boy!" the emo-kid shot back cheerily.

"Here," Phil said and handed the kid the black *Nightbreed* shirt. "This is the worst horror film ever made. It will be perfect to wipe your ass with while listening to that stupid fucking Uma Thurman dance song."

"Oh, I don't like that song," the kid said. "Only old Fall Out Boy. That is the real punk stuff, but not as good as Good Charlotte."

Phil started laughing right in his face. "You are the dumbest kid I ever met. If Glen Danzig heard you, he would grab you by your asymmetrical stupid-looking haircut and scalp you. Then he'd cum in your fucking brains, and light your head on fire, YOU STUPID FUCK!"

The kid's eyes grew wide and his lip started to tremble, until he was able to mutter, "Not Cool man. Not cool dude," and walked out of the store.

The boss slammed his fist on the counter and screamed, "That's it! You're fired, LoPresti! Go take your shit attitude and write a poem about what a fuck you are, then take a picture, and go sell it at the unemployment line. You fucking *stugotz!*"

"YOU FUCK! Fuck this place, fuck *Nightbreed,* and fuck Good Charlotte! I'd rather starve than sell these piece of shit t-shirts to a bunch of emo *fanooks!*"

LoPresti hated that job almost as much as he hated *Night-breed,* but when he looked at Facebook and saw the author of *The Premature Ejaculating Penises vs. The Alien Vaginas From Pluto Part 3* bragging in the thread that his book was in Amazon's top 10,000 book ranking, Phil felt hatred even greater for that book and its hack writer than he did for Barker's *Nightbreed.*

It repulsed him that these self-published hacks were destroying literature, one awful book at a time.

Though Phil didn't care for or want a traditional liberal arts education, he was more well-read than most MFA graduates, and believed his own poetry deserved recognition. He thought his photography was even better than his poetry, but most people on

Facebook would rather share memes than buy pictures of grave-yards, bloody crucifixes, and murky forests.

Phil looked away from the computer and peeked outside his smudged window. He saw trees in the breeze and thought about masturbating on them.

Since he hit puberty, the act of masturbating on trees had always given him an erotic euphoria akin to the darkly erotic poetry of Baudelaire. One review of his first book, *Haunted Fucking,* said LoPresti was a hybrid of Baudelaire and Bukowski.

Phil learned that great reviews did not sell books.

He looked back to his computer screen and decided he'd rather take his rage out on Facebook than ejaculate upon a birch tree.

He began typing out in all caps, "YOU FUCKS! I HAVE POETRY AND PHOTOGRAPHS FOR SALE AND YOU'D RATHER BUY TALKING PENIS BOOKS! DON'T YOU SEE I'M A GREAT GODDAMN ARTIST! NOT BECAUSE I'M THAT GREAT, BUT BECAUSE SO MANY BOOKS RIGHT NOW ARE SO FUCKING BAD. YOU SHOULD BE THANKING ME FOR CREATING ART THAT IS ACTUALLY DECENT!!!! I SHOULD QUIT WRITING SO YOU FUCKS CAN GO EAT YOUR QUINOA AND DRINK YOUR MICRO BREWS WHILE READING YOUR TALKING DICK VAGINA BOOKS UNTIL YOU CHOKE TO DEATH ON YOUR HIPSTER FOOD AND BEER. IF YOU HAVE ANY DECENCY AND HUMANITY, INSTEAD, YOU'D BUY MY LATEST BOOK WITH THE LINK AT THE BOTTOM. BUY IT YOU FUCKS!!!!!!!"

He posted the book link and looked to see if any person felt the same way or would *like* the comment and/or share the book link.

His writer friend, Christoph Paul, who was a decent guy, for a hack Jew writer, commented, "Why don't you say something political with menstrual blood, you know, like symbolism. The art scene might like that."

"That is FUCKING STUPID!" Phil typed back. "Why don't you and the art scene go DROWN IN MENSTRUAL BLOOD!"

Phil's post ended up only getting 6 *likes* from the same 6 people who always liked his posts because they found his rants ironically amusing. No one shared it.

He closed his computer and walked outside to find a tree to masturbate on.

Phil struggled to sleep later that night.

When sleep finally came, he dreamed he was reading at a coffeehouse open mic. He was performing a new poem from memory that mentioned menstrual blood coming from Jesus Christ's eyes.

Phil was surprised how good the poem was sounding.

He looked into the crowd to see the audience's responses, but saw no one was there except for two people sitting in a bed. They were two old white men with wrinkled naked bodies giving each other hand-jobs while reciting their own poetry.

Phil was about to curse them out, but he looked closer and saw that the old men were Charles Bukowski and Charles Baudelaire.

"What the fuck?" Phil said. "Show some fucking respect to a fan. I want you to hear my poems; you can jerk off each other's dicks afterwards."

"But we are dead, how can we hear you?" Dream Bukowski asked.

"You must read to the dying, that is where you will find and make art better than ourrrrrrrrrs," Baudelaire said in a ghostly tone, before ejaculating into the air.

Bukowski followed Baudelaire and ejaculated just as hard.

The cum floated in the air and then mixed together, like two white vines circling each other, until they became one. It kept twirling around until it stopped and formed a Japanese Haiku of semen.

Phil LoPresti couldn't read Japanese but he found it beautiful and knew what it meant in his heart.

The cum haiku gave him a reminder that he was a real artist but he had to suffer to make real art.

Phil tilted his head and nodded at the cum haiku. The semen poem hovered for a minute before splashing right into his face.

The dream facial woke him up screaming.

"What the hell, Phil?" said a half-awake Missy.

"I had a nightmare that was a prophetic vision about my poetry and the meaning of art."

"Oh Jesus," said Missy, flipping over, her legs tangling in the sheets.

"Fuck Jesus, real prophets spoke to me—Baudelaire and Bukowski. I know what I need to do for my art."

Missy yawned and said, "And what the hell is that, Phil?"

"Instead of watching Argento movies tomorrow I am going to the Cancer Ward at the hospital."

"Well, I guess that is a good thing to do. But what the hell are you planning to do there?"

"I am going to read my poems to the cancer patients and then take photographs of them while they contemplate oblivion."

"I'd rather you looked for a job," she said, turning back over.

2

PHIL WALKED INTO THE HOSPITAL WEARING BLACK LEVIS and a Misfits t-shirt of the same color. He signed in and a curvy black woman in a nursing outfit escorted him toward the entrance to the Cancer Ward. She was walking faster than him and gave him an annoyed look about his slow pace, but Phil was slowing down to check out her ass. He wasn't attracted to her, but he was an analingus enthusiast and believed that you could taste someone's soul by eating their asshole.

"Come on, move along, and stop staring at my shit," the orderly told Phil. "I know I'm a Kim K, I don't need your googly eyes to tell me what I already know."

"Sorry, I'm a poet."

"Yeah, yeah, so were two of my exes. *Poet* is just a fancy term for a nigga who doesn't like to pay the rent."

"Whatever," Phil said, shaking his head with annoyance.

"Don't you 'whatever' me. You just need to be real nice to these folks. They on their last breath. Hell, even some shitty poetry could be good for 'em."

"Yeah, I think my poetry can only be appreciated by the dying."

"Well, these people like seeing anyone, even poets."

Phil shook his head again and said, "Just take me to the cancer ward, Jesus fucking Christ. No respect."

The orderly put her key in the door and looked at Phil. "Hey, watch it with that shit. No cursing, especially around the old folks. They get uppity. Alright, now."

"Yeah, yeah, I have art to share with the dying."

The woman frowned and said, "You better not pull some bullshit, I'm serious, especially some weird-ass sex shit. I'll get the cops in a hot minute. I don't trust you creepy white boys wearing black t-shirts with weird shit on the front."

"It's *The Misfits!*"

"Don't you be one, or I'm calling the cops."

"Yeah, yeah, fine. Relax," Phil said and followed her through the doors of the Cancer Ward.

The smell of the Cancer Ward gave Phil a peaceful feeling.

There was something about being surrounded by death that relaxed him. He enjoyed contemplating about the beauty and fear of no longer existing, and loved to write poetry about how to deal with that simple but elegant truth.

He walked further into the Cancer Ward.

The floors were shiny and shoes squeaked with each step. He looked around and saw that most of the patients were asleep. He took a right and went into the recreational area, witnessing men and women of all ages with faces stripped of hope and joy.

Phil stood at the front of the room and asked, "So, who thinks they are going to die in the next couple of hours? I got something I want to read to you."

A frail old man raised his hand and said, "You can take your book of Jesus and shove it up your ass."

"I'm not a fucking Christian, I'm a poet," Phil responded.

"You're both fags!" the old man protested and laughed.

Phil walked over and said, "What are you, the fucking cancer comedian over here?"

"I'm not a comedian, but I am a death prophet," the old man said. "If you want to see death, look over at Robinson to your right. Yeah, the old negro that looks like a raisin with AIDS. He's gonna go in about 30 seconds maybe 35."

Phil looked into the old black's man eyes, they were half open but they were full of death.

"How do you know?"

"Cause I've been in this ward for 3 years. I've had three different kinds of cancer but none of them took me yet. I've been battling death so long that I can smell it when it's ready. Death got a smell too. Dogs know it. They'll turn their back on you when death is in you and ready to take ya for good. Death comes and leaves you with a big shit in your pants and unfinished dreams in your heart."

"That's fucking poetry."

"Words aren't real poetry, but what's about to happen to Robinson is," the old man said, his eyes fixed on the black man.

Phil and he watched Robinson's eyes roll back and black shit-water drip down his chair.

Robinson's body went limp.

He tumbled over, falling into the shit puddle.

The old man shook his head and said, "Colon cancer. They always have the diarrhea shits when they go."

Phil stared at the shitty liquid leaving the old man's body and traveling through the title cracks like little brown snakes being born. "God damn, this really is poetry. I'm never writing another poem again! Art's fucking dead."

"Nothing is dead but people," the old man said. "You want to make real art. Something that will speak to people?"

"Yes, that is the only reason why I haven't killed myself...well that and Missy."

"You need to show the opposite of death, you need to show history and its wars. You need to remind us why we are even here. Show nature in its brutality and majesty."

Phil nodded and then paused to reflect and said, "Menstrual blood."

The old man smiled and showed missing and rotten teeth. "You like menstrual blood, eh?"

"What?"

"Answer me!"

"Yeah, most of my poems are about it. How did you know?"

"I can smell it on you, you like to lick the pussy blood. I can tell."

"Fuck, what are you, a prophet?"

"No, but I smell life as much as death. Truth seekers know menstrual blood holds great truth. It is the decay of life, but life is decay."

"Fuck! That is totally true! I wish you were my dad! You're like a bedridden Bukowski."

"Don't compare me to that commie degenerate!"

"Sorry, it was compliment," Phil said. "So what should I do?

"You must show this in real art, not in your pointless poems. Show them the power of the menstrual blood. Show them how tainted we all have become and we need be cleansed."

"I'll do it." Phil said with reverence. "I'll go home right now, make it, and present it at the art show in Montclair. I'll come back and tell you if I won. I'll even split the prize money with you."

"No you won't."

"Why? You are cool! You are the artistic mentor I've been needing and looking for."

"No, because I won't be here."

"Where the fuck are you going?"

"To oblivion. I smell my own death, it's coming in 14 maybe 15 hours."

"YOU FUCK!" Phil said. "Thanks for abandoning me."

"Death is already here for me. It is natural and good. I welcome death."

"Alright fine," Phil said, "at least I get to keep all the prize money."

Phil walked out of the Cancer Ward and tiptoed down the hall, reaching the janitor's room. He looked around to make sure no one was coming and snuck inside. He found cleaning supplies and the *New Jersey Times* on the floor, but he smiled, seeing the door leading to the trash heap outside.

"Score!" He said and grabbed a pair of gloves on the desk and two trash bags. He cracked his knuckles and opened the back door, and walked outside toward the dumpster.

He climbed over the metal edge and jumped inside. The smell of used bedpans made him nauseous. He held his nose and spotted a bag. It was white with blots of red spreading inside of it. Phil ripped the trash bag open. An old *People Magazine* with Farrah Abrams on the cover dropped to the ground with a couple of bloody tampons on her face.

Phil found the image poetic.

The smell was putrid but Phil didn't mind suffering for his art. He started scooping out all of the used tampons. The menstrual blood was the baby that would never be born and that was poetry to Phil.

Phil thought about what his Facebook friend, Christoph Paul would think of his menstrual political art photography piece. He hated to admit it, but that stupid Jew was right about him needing to get more political and shock the art community. He also thought that it was pretty fucking stupid for a Jew to be named Christoph, but life was pretty stupid and pointless.

Phil threw the used tampons into the trash bag, but saw there were still a few bloody tampons on the ground. He kneeled down to pick them up but noticed a shadow obscuring his view.

"Oh, help me, Jesus!" the voice in the shadow screamed. Phil turned around and saw the orderly starring at him with disgust.

"Shit!" screamed Phil.

"Aw hell no," the orderly said. "I knew I shouldn't have let you in. I knew something was off. You probably gonna get freaky with them tampons. Oh Jesus, you testing me too much these days. Too damn much, Lord!"

"It's ... for art..." said Phil.

She grabbed a broom stick and screamed, "And this is for Jesus!" as she swung the stick at him. Phil ducked the blow and ran away carrying his trash bag full of used tampons.

3

Phil ran as far as he could from the South Jersey Care Hospital.

He hauled his trash bag of used Tampons and made it five blocks from the hospital, before he was out of breath. He started heaving and coughing and his stomach growled. The street was dirty and hot. The dust clung to his skin. His hair swept over his eyes as the sweat dripped down. There were cigarette butts all over the ground. He reached inside of his pocket for cigarettes but they were all gone.

"Shit," said Phil, realizing they had fallen out at the hospital.

He looked up the block and saw a Subway. Italian subs were Phil's favorite meal, but he usually ate homemade ones. He didn't have any money for sandwiches or cigarettes, but he had an idea.

He walked into the Subway, catching a whiff of the fresh baked bread. He hoped it would conceal the smell of the tampons. The store was empty except for a Pakistani man standing behind the counter, warming up some Italian multi-grain bread.

"Yes, young man," the Subway manager said with a thick accent. "How may I help you?"

"Yeah, I'm here for the free footlong. Get me an Italian sub."

The man looked confused. He scratched his beard and said, "Sandwich is not free. No free sandwiches."

"Bullshit, it's not. I ate a ton of your Italian subs not knowing I was supporting a pedophile. Subway fucking duped me. I am now addicted to your Italian subs, and my money went to that creepy fuck buying Swedish child porn."

"I am very sorry, sir. I no know the Jared. I think the Jared is disgusting," the man said gravely. "In Pakistan we would have fed him his own scrotum."

"At least Pakistan has their priorities right," Phil replied. "I fucking hate pedos. I would starve them to death, and then I'd peel off their skin like potatoes and feed it back to those FUCKS."

"That is what will happen to the Jared in the afterlife. I have son too, young boy, because American schools so bad I sent him to a Catholic Charter school, but that school not good either, but at least there are no Jews there. If anything happened to my dear boy I would destroy them."

"Too bad Jared got to eat so many free Subways. He probably ate meatball subs while looking at kiddie porn. THAT PISSES ME THE FUCK OFF!"

"My soul is angered as well, young man," said the owner. "I'm a man of honor and when I learned of the Jared I was deeply sad. Before I moved here, I saw the commercials of the Jared looking so happy, no longer being fat, and I knew right then and there that America was great place. I am very sad now, I was fooled by the American dream and the Jared, and my business is doing no good these days."

"Why? Do people think they'll become pedos by eating at Subway?"

"I don't know," said the Subway manager. He looked around and said in a lower voice. "It is not just the Jared, it is also the Mafia."

Phil laughed and said, "Why would the Mafia give a shit about Subway?"

"We didn't pay their fees for protection and now they have hot dog salesmen everywhere. They see weakness in Subway shop, so they set up their hot dog stands all around our stores."

"Fuck, I didn't know the sandwich industry was so brutal and cutthroat."

"Look, I make you deal. I give you free sandwich, but you promise that you never buy hot dogs or work for these *burrai* hot doggers. The hot dog Mafia, very bad for sandwich business and for America."

"Yeah, I fucking hate hot dogs. It's food for *fanooks*."

"You give me your word."

"Yeah, what the fuck do I care? I give you my word."

"Very good, my friend. I will make you the meatball sub on the house."

Phil smiled and watched him make the sub, thinking how he and the Pakistani man were both good men who were being fucked over by the system.

Phil thought it really was about time for him to get political and say something in his art.

Phil sat down at the dinner table, put on some yellow rubber gloves, and took the stolen tampons out of the black trash bag as soon as he got home. Laid out on the table were pictures and photographs of different travesties from the last two centuries, along with Photoshopped abortion photos pasted upon a large inspirational poster about Perseverance. A month ago Phil had stolen the poster from an H&R Block because they couldn't help him write off Missy's tampons and his horror Blu-Ray DVD collection as business expenses.

Phil picked up his glue stick, ready to make his masterpiece for the Montclair Photo-Art Show, but he heard a knock at the door.

"I'm making art, YOU FUCKS! Leave me alone!"

"Phil, I just need to hide from the bullies," the voice of a young boy begged behind his door. "Please Phil. Please. Let me in!"

Phil recognized the voice.

It was his neighbor, Dan, a redheaded stepchild who got beat up all time. Even though Phil thought Dan was a *meza fanook*, he saw him as a decent kid. Phil yelled at the door, "Alright fine, but nothing is free, YOU FUCK! You got to help glue these bloody tampons wherever I tell you."

"Whatever you want! Please! Just let me in Phil, I can't take another wedgie."

"Fucking pussy. Alright, hold on," Phil said, leaving his pile of used Tampons and opened up the door, "Come on, hurry up. I got world-changing art to make, and money to win!"

"Thanks Phil, you're a life saver," the young boy said, and ran inside.

Little Dan looked right at the table and saw Phil wasn't kidding.

The young boy didn't know much about menstruation, but he was scared of blood.

Phil picked up an extra pair of gloves from under the kitchen skin, and threw them at the kid. "Alright Dan, find the ones that are the least bloody and place them on the top of the poster near the fetus pictures."

Dan was freaked out by all the tampons, but it was better than being outside. He still was unsure why Phil had so many bloody tampons on his kitchen table, but he was willing to do whatever Phil said.

Dan started gluing them to the Perseverance poster. "It must be so cool to be a talented artist, Phil."

Phil kept on pasting the bloody tampons to the poster. "Don't say such fucking nonsense. Being a real artist is just a life of misery, poverty, and hatred."

"It sounds like middle school."

"IT'S WORSE!"

"I don't want to make art ever again!"

Philip looked up from the bloody mess. "I am happy to hear that. You'll probably have less misery in your life. But for now, let's paste these bloody tampons in the middle and then add the pictures of Jared that FUCK from Subway along with screen-shots of *Nightbreed*."

Phil finished the art project a few hours after Dan snuck home for dinner. He hid the artwork in the pantry because he knew Missy would yell at him. She had called earlier to say she was working the late shift at the diner.

Phil was alone with his laptop opened to Facebook. He watched other writers share their books and get all kinds of praise and attention, congratulating each other on their books, even though Phil was pretty sure it was all just a bunch of masturbatory hipster crap.

Phil needed something to go right.

Missy was sick of him being unemployed and no one was buying his poetry books.

He needed a break.

He shook his head and typed, "ALL YOUR BOOKS SUCK! NONE OF THEM ARE REAL ART! TOMORROW REAL ART AND BRILLIANCE WILL BE REWARDED. THE CREAM WILL RISE TO THE TOP AND DROWN ALL YOUR MEDIOCRE WORK THAT BELONGS UP THE ASSHOLE OF THE MANAGER OF URBAN OUTFITTERS! IF YOU WANT TO SEE REAL ART COME OUT TOMORROW TO THE MONTCLAIR ART AND PHOTOGRAPHY CONTEST! I'LL BE PRESENTING MY BEST WORK THAT IS A MILLION TIMES BETTER THAN ALL OF YOUR SHIT ART COMBINED AND IT'S FREE SO COME OUT YOU CHEAP ASS FUCKING FUCKS!!!"

4
___

PHIL ARRIVED AT THE MONTCLAIR ART MUSEUM WITH HIS art project covered in a white cloth. He walked through the wide double doors. Inside it smelled of potpourri and the wall was covered with pictures of deceased New Jersey artists and photographers. There was a sign that said "Art & Photography Contest in the Left Wing. Free. Complimentary Cheese and Comedy Host."

Phil went to the Left Wing.

It had high ceilings and looked like a large art instillation. It was all white with chairs in rows of eight. There was a small raised stage at the back of the room. To the left of the stage was a small table of complimentary cheese. Phil grabbed two pounds worth of sharp cheddar. He took his plate of cheese and found a seat in the back row.

He looked around, disappointed about the meager turnout. There was barely anyone under forty-five in the audience. The old people looked like they were dressed for a funeral being held at the Golden Corral. Most of them looked bored and ready to fall asleep.

Phil ate cheese and fidgeted in his seat. He was pissed that he couldn't light up a cigarette during the show. He kept looking down at his project, worried that the blood would seep through.

A man who was bald and fat wearing a green suit two sizes too small stepped onto the stage. Phil shook his head, wondering who's this stupid fuck that looked like Leisure Suit Larry.

The frumpy man smiled and wiped sweat off his large oily forehead with a napkin from the cheese table. "Hey everyone, welcome to the Montclair Art and Photography Contest. What a show we got here, folks, what a show. There is gonna be some great art here, my wife can't call me a philistine anymore unless we visit Palestine, but Israel won't let that happen, cause my wife is a Jew ..."

No one laughed and the comedian said, "Oy vey, tough crowd. What are you going to do? My wife isn't doing me ... ok, ok. Tough crowd. Alright, let's get started. First up we got a young man who defines himself as Neo-Alt-Lit named Steve Hoggenbuck."

Phil chewed on his fingernails and watched a chubby white male twenty-something, dressed in a grey sweatshirt that said *#hashtag*, step onto the stage. Phil shook his head in disgust and said loudly, "Fucking hipster posers. They should all get shot."

When people turned around with annoyance, he just shrugged.

The hipster kid nodded his head shyly and unveiled his artwork. It was all screenshots of his own Facebook statuses. They were the ones that got the most *likes*.

Hoggenbuck smiled and said, "I'm a Neo-Alt-Lit writer and this is my art. Books are no longer the canvas. They are the trees and should stay that way. The Internet is the new tree ... of life ... but way better than that movie. As you can see, my status 'i stop for dogs but they stop to bark,' really captures the vibe of what it means to be human, because as you can see from the 322 *likes*, this message really resonated with people."

Phil looked at the judges as they nodded thoughtfully.

"What the fuck is this nonsense," he said and yelled,

"Bukowski would jerk off and puke all over this! Total garbage. Just give me the winner money now. I'm the only person with any talent in this damn room."

The comedian host cringed for a second but forced out a smile.

He walked up on stage and said, "I think this young man in the crowd is not alt-lit, but more like ... angry lit. Are there any writers here in Anger Management classes? Man, I'd hate to be their editor, amiright?"

The crowd was still not laughing.

Halfway through the show, the comedian was covered in sweat. "Tough crowd, tough crowd, but not as tough as young Bukowski over there. Speaking of, it is time we meet our next artist. He is a photographer and a poet and his books ... whoa, I can't even name any of these titles. Alright Philip LoPresti, come on up and show us what you got."

Phil heard a few polite claps as he brought the cloth-covered poster to the stage. He surveyed the sea of scowling old people. *God damn it*, he thought, *a free art show and the youth of America is too busy playing video games, Tweeting, and fingering each other's buttholes to take time for real art. Fuck them, I hope they all die of ass cancer.*

Phil looked away from the crowd and back to his poster. He picked it up gingerly, and placed it on the art frame. The cloth clung to the bloody tampons and little red dots soon became blotches.

Phil turned back toward the crowd and said, "What you saw earlier by Steve Hoggenbuck was an abortion. Alt-Lit in any form is a Holocaust of art. Anything with alt in the title is ignorant, hackneyed, and fucking stupid."

He stared down Hoggenbuck, who was live-Tweeting about how a neo-Bukowski was a crazy Anti-Neo-Alt-Liter. "Seriously, this guy, Steve Hoggenbuck, is the Joseph Goebbels of art. You are all fools, looking into the blinding sun that reflects off your hipster and old people glasses. You need real art to help you see again. So, behold!" Phil took off the white sheet and the entire crowd gasped.

He smiled as every mouth dropped in disgust at the Perseverance poster that had been transformed into a De Sadesque collage from Hell.

There were lurid images of aborted fetuses that had joker smiles painted on their heads. On their chests, each had a Photoshopped tattoo that said, "I'm Happy, I'm Dead, I Feel Nothing." On each of their heads, there were four bloody tampons laid out in the shape of the cross. In the middle of the Perseverance poster was a smiling picture of Jared from Subway. Next to Jared were different scenes from *Nightbreed* that were cut and pasted together, forming a giant phallus. The *Nightbreed* phallus shot out sperms with screaming Macaulay Culkin faces. They were heading straight at the smiling Jared.

Phil nodded his head with pride, but the old people started gagging and crying. An old woman in the front put her hand on her heart, screamed, and fell out of her chair onto floor.

Her face went blue and the white pants she wore turned brown.

Steve Hoggenbuck was throwing up and he kept throwing up until he was dry heaving. He wiped his mouth, and said, "Your awful art ... it ... it killed her."

The old man next to her held his nose and put his ear to her chest.

"She doesn't have a heartbeat. Call 9-1 1."

Phil got home later that night. Missy was lying on her stomach on top of their bed. Her long brown hair was in a bun. She was wearing a white shirt without a bra, cotton panties, and was reading *A Dance with Dragons*. Phil stared at her ass; it always made him feel better about the horrors of existence.

"Hey babe, how did the art contest go? You look sort of happy, and sort of shocked. Did you win?"

"No, but I see now that I truly am a special artist."

Miss sighed and said, "Phil, I really do believe in you as an artist, I do, but I really need you to become more conscious about money. You are a great photographer but you probably put up pictures of fetuses, and god knows what for this contest."

"Art is more important than money, Missy!" said Phil. "Art can affect both life and death. I saw that tonight, and in a weird way I'm proud of myself. I mean I feel sort of bad, but it was an old lady—I saved her from suffering and probably cancer."

"What the hell are you talking about, Phil?"

"This old lady died after seeing my art project. I mean, I feel bad she died but Missy, that shows that I really know how to make true art!"

"Stop fucking me with Phil. It's not funny."

"I'm not kidding. She shit herself and everything. My art literally killed her," he exclaimed, beaming.

Missy stared at him, flabbergasted. "And you're proud of this?"

"Look, I am not a psychopath, I said I am sad the lady died, but yeah I am kind of proud. Real art should kill a few people!"

"Go sleep on the fucking couch. I can't even look at you," said Missy, slamming the George R.R. Martin book on their bed.

"What the hell, Missy! You could be more supportive."

"Get the fuck out of the room and go to the couch. You want support go ask Facebook for it. I can't believe you, Phil."

"Fine, I will," said Phil, leaving the room and going to his well-worn spot on the couch.

He picked up his laptop and logged into Facebook. In his absence, he had been tagged a total of 57 times and had 140 notifications.

"Fuck," said Phil, closing his computer. He stared out his window into the blackness, contemplating the desolation of the universe for four hours.

5

PHIL HAD ALWAYS WANTED TO SEE HIMSELF IN THE newspaper for his art, but he felt sad seeing the headline, "Terror Artist Kills Elderly Woman with Offensive Art, Her Children Are Devastated."

Missy usually enjoyed reading the morning paper before an early shift, but not today.

"God damn it, Phil," said Missy. She put down the newspaper and finished her coffee. "I don't know what makes me more disgusted with you, that you stole used tampons and put them on a poster board of fetus pictures, or that you are proud that your art killed some poor old woman."

Phil exhaled a drag of his first Marlboro of the day, ate another spoonful of Cheerios, and said, "That was before I knew she had foster kids who were young. I genuinely feel bad. Yeah, I sort of like that my art can kill people, but I feel sad as fuck for those kids."

Phil felt no real guilt for killing a philistine old lady, but he was upset for leaving foster kids without a mom. Phil's mom had died when he was young and if he had any soft spot, it was for children who had to survive tragedy.

"You should be upset that you caused someone's death," Missy shot back.

"Oh, whatever Missy. Before the days of Christianity and Häagen-Dazs, people would have praised me for killing someone with my art. Pagans would praise me."

"That is ridiculous, Phil! Life was never like that!"

"Yes it was!"

"When? When the hell was that Phil?"

"I'm pretty sure the Egyptians were like that. They appreciated art! And even the Mexicans, you know, like before the Spaniards came over and raped them."

"Phil shut up, you failed History class junior year."

"Yeah, because that teacher was a cunt and hated me."

"You called her a retarded twat in class, Phil."

"Yeah, well she said Bukowski wasn't an important part of American History. That is the dumbest fucking shit I have ever heard!"

Missy fired back, "Phil, can you please just take responsabili...." but was cut off by a knock at the door.

"Hello, is the resident Philip LoPresti home?" a voice behind their door asked.

"Fuck you! I'm not home," Phil said.

"Um ... sir ..."

"Get the fuck out of here! I don't want to speak to the god damn media?"

"Sir, I'm not the media, I'm from the courts."

Phil walked outside, lit up a cigarette, and said, "What the fuck do you want? Wait, do I have court duty? Actually, that would be good. I need the money. I'll do court duty if it is over a week."

"Um, no man," said the thirty-something chubby guy with old school headphones around his neck and a Metalocalypse t-shirt.

He handed Phil a letter and said, "You are being sued by Mr. Thorogood and his family estate."

"The fucking blues singer? Ah fuck, I am sampled that 'I Drink Alone' song years ago. I quit music. I'm only doing poetry and photography now. That old fuck must be hard up for money if he wants to sue my ass."

"No, not *George Thorogood and The Destroyers*. Decent band, though, but not brutal enough for me, but no, it's the old woman's family. Dude, you know you are in the paper. It's pretty brutal what you did."

"What the fuck? How can they sue? That's fascist."

"I don't know bro. I mean, I'm sad for the family and all that, but it is pretty brutal that you killed someone with your art."

"Hell yeah it is!"

"Sorry I have to give you this, but I got to pay the bills man and day job it. I'm an artist too; I play bass and back-up vocals in the Desert Rock Death Metal Band *Benzos and Buttholes*. It's brutal stoner metal."

"That sounds fucking awful, no offense, the only band I like is *Swans*."

"Fair enough man."

"What's not fair is artists like us are treated like criminals and we have to work jobs that are fucking pointless. It's a modern fucking travesty," said Phil, lighting another cigarette.

"I hear ya man, I wrote this song about all the shitty shit, man. Let me sing it to you it before I go."

The man pretended to play bass and sang in cookie monster sounding vocals:

Third Trimester little babies
    I can see they got the rabies
    They bite, they bite
    They bite, they bite
    THEY BITE YOUR FREEDOM AWAY!!!

Wedding bells ring so loud
    One's enough but two's a crowd
    They fight, they fight
    They fight, they fight
    FOR THAT MOTHER FUCKING BOUQUET!!!

"That's actually pretty good," Phil said, "I never want to get married; stupid fucking bullshit, just like having a day job."

The metal process server shook his head and whispered, "Dude, behind you..."

Phil turned around and saw Missy with her arms crossed, looking even angrier.

"You've been served," the metal-lover said, leaving the court papers by Phil's feet.

Phil followed Missy back inside. She took out another

cigarette and lit it up. Phil shook his head about how fucked he was and took another big drag. He exhaled and said, "I didn't mean it. I would marry you, I just don't have my shit together, so it scares the fuck out of me."

"Well, I don't want to marry a guy who has no job and steals bloody tampons from hospitals," said Missy, grabbing the court document from him. "Let me see what this."

Half way through reading it she coughed out smoke and said, "They are suing you ... for fucking money, Phil! Money we don't have!"

"What? Ha," Phil laughed. "They won't win, I'll get some Jew lawyer from the state and he'll talk about the First Amendment. I'll be fine."

"No, it won't be fine, Phil! Jesus, there is always something. Always some ridiculous bullshit we have to deal with because of you thinking you're a serious artist, and like usual, you don't take any consequences seriously. And that hurt ... it hurt what you said to that stupid guy."

"I didn't mean it. I love you, Missy."

Missy hated how much she loved Phil and she hated herself because she always ended up forgiving him. She was a good Southern Girl who believed in tradition, but love made her stay with the most untraditional man she ever met.

"I love you too, Phil ... I just wish ... you'd get your shit together."

"I'm trying Missy. It's just ... this world is so fucked and they don't appreciate real artists and all ..."

Missy slammed her fist on the table. "Jesus Christ, Phil, just take some responsibility. You always, every god damn time blame everyone else, but you never take time to look into your own bullshit."

"All serious artists get attacked by society. That's how it's always been."

"Oooh poor Phil, he's a real artist, boo fucking hoo. Why

don't we hold a telethon for Phil, the poor menstruation loving photo-taking poet."

"They should. If A&E had integrity they would do a special on my work!"

"We might need a telethon if you lose the case."

"I'm not going to lose. Don't be ridiculous."

"You might!"

"Whatever," said Phil, feeling nervous that maybe he would. "Can you come to court with me the day of trail?"

"No, I have to work, Phil."

PART 2

6

Philip LoPresti sat in a small and dusty South Jersey courtroom. It was truly a depressing place. Our Lady of Justice hovered in the back, her head covered in spider webs. Next to Phil was a volunteer public defender assigned to his civil case.

Phil brushed the dust off the brown oversize suit that his Fat Uncle Sal had loaned him. The state had given him a Chinese lawyer, while the Thorogoods had a lawyer so Jewey, Phil swore he could smell the pastrami sandwich he had eaten for lunch.

The night before he had also Googled his judge and learned that he was a proud member of the PMRC. Wikipedia also mentioned that Judge Roberts was still friends with Tipper Gore and was known for going to all you can eat buffets with Chris Christie.

Apparently Judge Roberts had once said that the only good artists were the one who designed the American Flag and the directors behind the film *Independence Day*.

Judge Roberts looked just as angry as he did in his Wikipedia picture. He shot a look of disdain to Phil and then turned his attention on the prosecutor and said, "Mr. Kurshner, please proceed."

"Don't worry, Mr. LoPresti," Phil's lawyer whispered in his right ear. "DeVry University taught me very well."

Phil chewed his fingernails and said under his breath, "I'm so fucked."

Mr. Kurshner stood up, smiled at the judge and said, "Thank you, Judge Roberts. This case is important to me. I am a follower of the news of domestic and foreign terrorism. Do you know that ISIS is starting to teach their young boys in the mosque to make ... terrorist art? It's true. They are realizing that creativity in the hands of angry men can be a powerful weapon. These terrorist artists, or terror-artists, are trying to find their way out of the Middle East and into this great country. LoPresti might be a homegrown terror-artist, but like ISIS, he is out to cause terror and bring death to good Americans."

"You gotta be fucking kidding me, this guy is like the cousin of *Better Call Saul*," Phil protested.

Judge Roberts slammed his gravel. "Another peep out of you Mr. LoPresti and you'll be in contempt ... continue, Mr. Kurshner."

"Thank you, judge. Terrorism is serious as, well, a heart attack," said Mr. Kurshner, pausing as one of the adopted children of the Thorogoods began to cry. "As you can see and hear, it causes tragedy, causes heartache, causes loss. And God bless her soul, Mrs. Thorogood was a victim of artistic terrorism. That poor woman's family is now suffering because of Philip LoPresti's terror-art. Now, I know you can't charge him for murder or manslaughter, but there was clear antagonism. Clear intent to make an innocent hearts come to a tragic stop. Intent to harm and it do. His terror art caused a poor woman to reach her death much to soon, and the suffering family from this disaster deserves to be compensated. Judge Roberts, you can look at Mr. LoPresti and the see the callous ways in his eyes. He wasn't making art ... he was destroying the innocent."

The Judge nodded without even bothering to look impartial. "Thank you, Mr. Kurshner. Very well said. I am sorry that Mr.

LoPresti interrupted. Alright Mr. Chang, please give us your defense statement."

The frumpy lawyer nodded and said, "Your honor I would like to bring Philip LoPresti to stand."

Phil walked to the stand and sat down. He tried his best to look remorseful, but he could feel the families and judge's eye staring at him.

Phil forced himself to sit up and his lawyer held up a picture of his artwork and asked, "Mr. LoPresti, was this the art project you created with the intent to shock others so much they could harmed?"

The judged cringed and waved his hand to cover it up.

"Sorry to show that you judge, it would make the Marquis De Sade blush," said the prosecutor.

Phil wanted to thank the prosecutor for the compliment, but he noticed the angry look on the judge's face. "I'm under oath, so I can't lie, right?"

"You will be in contempt of court and go to jail if you lie under oath," Judge Roberts responded.

"Damn it, ok ... then, um, yeah. I make art to hurt people, but only their soul."

"Their soul?" asked Lawyer Chang.

"Yeah, not physically, I just want them to question their will to live, like any real artist does."

Lawyer Chang looked as worried as Phil, and said, "Ok. No more questions. That is all your honor ... um, I would like to approach the bench."

After a half hour of deliberation and talks of a plea bargain, Judge Roberts was ready to hear the final statements and said, "Mr. Kurshner, you may go first."

The lawyer nodded to Judge Roberts and said, "So, Mr. LoPresti creates art to tempt people to take their life, or so they feel so overwhelmed by Existential grief that their heart stops beating like poor Mrs. Thorogood's. Well that heart, it had many more beats left in it, but Phillip LoPresti's art stopped it and crushed the hearts of a good-hearted family, and even in their grief they don't wish harm on LoPresti. The least he could do is pay for their funeral bills. I'm not a judge like you sir, I'm just a nice Jewish boy who grew up in South Carolina and now has a family in Jersey, but where I come from, well ... we just do what is right. Mr. LoPresti should have offered to pay for the funeral and not have us all wasting our time here today."

"I'm sorry for their loss, but this is bullshit..." Phil retorted.

The judge slammed his gavel and said, "Mr. LoPresti, I warned you."

"Sorry."

"No, judge I'm sorry," said Mr. Kurshner. "I feel sorry for Mr. LoPresti. That is alright, I think that outburst shows the truth in Mr. LoPresti's heart. Thank you your honor. That is all."

"Thank you, Mr. Kurshner," the judge said. "Mr. Chang you may now present your closing argument."

"That is ok judge, I do not have one."

"A fair and wise choice Mr. Chang," the judge responded.

"What the hell!" Phil screamed. "This is a goddamn mockery of the justice system, Jesus Christ!"

The judge slammed his gravel and said, "Mr. LoPresti, I hold both of those holy names dear to my heart ... my goodness, I've heard enough. This is turning into a carnival freak show. I've reached my decision. Mr. LoPresti will have to pay for the funeral, which amounts to three-thousand, and two-hundred and sixty-two dollars. Mr. LoPresti will have to pay that exact amount in 90 days or he will be sent to jail. That is my verdict and it is final."

Phil walked out of the courthouse and down its wide front grey steps.

His head was down and his shoulders were slumped in a way that made his Fat Cousin Sal's brown suit look even worse. He took his favorite Nikon camera out of his pocket, pointed it at his face, and screamed, "FUCCCCKKKK!" and took a picture.

He lit up a cigarette and heard the word 'fuck' screamed seconds later.

It sounded like an echo, but it wasn't his voice.

He looked around and saw a hot dog stand in front of an alleyway with no one tending it. He heard more screams coming from the back alley behind the hot dog stand.

Cigarette dangling from his mouth and his camera in hand, he walked past the hot dog-stand and down the alley toward the sound.

It smelled like piss and garbage. The screaming had stopped and Phil saw three wise guys wearing suits that what were much nicer than his. Behind them laid a dead fat man sprawled out on the ground. The puddle of his blood flowed down to their shoes.

The wise guys looked up at Phil, as he took his last drag and thought, *fuck, well I hope Haunted Fucking at least gets read by more than 100 people now*, and stood there, waiting for death.

The mafiosos walked toward Phil. The tallest one who looked familiar and in his fifties said, "Hey kid, fucking tragic over here. You see where the *mullion* went who did this to this poor hot dog salesman? Look at this poor dead fat fuck. It's disrespectful what these *mullies* do, fucking tragic."

The man then smiled and the others approached while making sure not to get blood on their shoes.

Phil stared at the dead man and noticed three hot dogs stuffed inside the fat man's mouth. "Nah, I saw you guys ..." Phil stopped and realized what they wanted him to say. "I mean ... oh ... yeah, yeah, fucking *mulli*, he totally did it. Though, you say 'black guy' now ... but... yeah, I saw a black guy do it."

"Smart kid," the tall mobster said.

Phil recognized him. He was Dean Martino, the head of the Martino Crime Family and said, "Nah, but I'm smart enough to mind my own business."

"Like I said, smart kid. Why aren't you at work or in college? What are you on a lunch break? Or are you..." Dean Martino asked, but stopped seeing the camera in Phil's hand. "What the fuck are you, FBI ... what the fuck are you carrying that camera around for?"

The men took out their guns and pointed them at Phil.

Phil felt his anus clench. He shook his head and said, "I'm not a cop, FBI, or criminal or nothing. I'm just a poet and photographer. I swear! I just got out of court. I gotta pay a bunch of money because one of my photos made an old lady die. I shoot transgressive photography, that's it. I'm no fucking Fed, I swear to ya, I'm not a liar!"

"A photographer of fucked up stuff, huh," Dean Martino said, lowering his gun and scratching his chin with it. "So you owe some money, huh, kid. From the look of your piece of shit suit you won't be able to pay it...it looks like you need a job." Martino smiled again and asked, "You want one working for us?"

"I'll do anything except give handjobs or watch *Nightbreed*."

"*Nightbreed*?" The mafia boss asked, and looked at the two *goombas* next to him for answers. "What the fuck is a *Nightbreed*?"

The *pisan* to Dean Martino's left shrugged, but a man to his right with a ponytail and goatee said, "It's some movie with a bunch of *fanooks* wearing facepaint. Ugh, forget about it, it's no *Goodfellas*."

"Enough of this nonsense," the mafia boss said, turning back to Phil. "You look like a decent *pisan*, and we need a new kid to work the hot dog stand and do photo stuff."

"You want me to sell hot dogs?"

"Yeah, and you say you're a photographer, well good, cause what you'll do is sell some hot dogs, eat a few if you like, and look for cars around here. If you see people parking for more than 5 minutes you take pictures of their plates, and every once in a while there will be a guy who will come by. He will want you to take some pictures. It will be for a specific job. It will be for some real money."

"How much?"

"Fifty dollars an hour, and for the photography gigs, three thousand."

"Shit," Phil said. "I could pay off the courts by the end of the week. Are you fucking serious?"

"Look at the fat fuck on the ground and ask me if I'm serious again."

Phil nodded that he understood the Don, but told him, "I don't believe in most laws or morality, but I don't do drugs or sell them. People need to feel the pain of existence."

"Hey, you weird fuck, this isn't a fucking Sopranos sequel

audition. I'm not some *mulli* and this isn't the fucking Wire. No fucking drugs. All you do is sell some hot dogs and take some fucking pictures. You're some artsy *meza fanook*, well guess what, you're gonna get to be one of the few lucky ones who gets paid doing what they love to do. Don't take a gift horse in the mouth, kid."

"Ok, ok. When do I start?"

"When the fuck do you think? Right the fuck now. We need someone manning that hot dog stand. We are already losing customers."

7

PHIL LoPRESTI STOOD BY THE HOT DOG STAND IN HIS oversized suit.

"Hey, you fucks, want some hot dogs ... hey old lady, come on, buy a hot dog, they're good," he said as people walked by, taking a savage bite out of a freshly heated hot dog.

But no one bought anything.

Phil shook his head and said, "Fucking ingrates, if we were in Korea those fucks would be lining up. They eat real fucking dogs. Everything is too easy in this goddamn country."

He took out another hot dog and put some mustard on it. He ate the hot dog in three bites. He felt inspired to write a poem.

He grabbed a napkin and wrote:

> *The dogs we eat are hot dog abortions*
> *made in Chinese sweat shops.*
>
> *The dumplings are cooked in the cum*
> *of Geese*
> *whose wings*
> *were clipped*

and the necks
are hung like slaves
beside the raped ghosts
of the gluttonous
who deserve a fist
up their soul's rectal inactivity...

... A loud knock and voices cursing in a foreign accent stopped Phil from finishing the poem.

"What the fuck, YOU FUCKS! I'm writing a poem about the disenchantment of being a hot dog salesman! This better be important!"

Phil looked up and saw the Pakistani Subway owner who had gave him the free Italian Subway. Two angry men, also wearing Subway uniforms and long beards accompanied him.

They both gave Phil the finger and the man he met before said, "No! You are the fuck! You were spying on us. You are part of the hot dog Mafia ... we are at war with you Italians. You try to charge us rent and then sell hot dogs to hurt our business. Terrible! Allah shall punish you, I spit on your hot dogs. It is devil meat. May they spoil like your soul, *Inshallah*."

All three men began spitting on the hot dogs.

"Hey, stop that!" Phil said. "Don't spit on my fucking hot dogs. At least the mafia doesn't employ child molesters like that sick fuck Jared."

Phil took out his tongs and pinched one guy's nose as he squirted mustard into the other one's eyes.

The two men screamed and ran way, but the owner stayed and said, "You are a traitor and you broke your word."

Phil looked the Subway manager in his eyes and said, "Man to man, I'm sorry. I broke my promise but I had no choice. I seriously had no fucking choice. They would have killed me. I had to do it."

"I came to this country to have more choice, more freedom,

but instead of the Mullahs, now I have to deal with the hot dog mafia," the Subway manager said and then walked away.

The hours passed and Phil ate his seventh hot dog of the day.

"These hot dogs are pretty fucking good," Phil said to himself, as he finished it in four bites and wiped his hand on his grimy jeans.

He lit up a cigarette, inhaled and exhaled, wondering why no matter how hard or little he tried, he always wound up in situations where he had to fuck someone over to not get fucked. He didn't feel much guilt or sadness about the dead old woman or the fat man he found in the alley, but he did feel guilty for breaking his word to the Subway owner.

Phil took another drag and watched a few boys in Catholic school uniforms walk past the hot dog stand. Seeing them took him back to his first moment of misanthropy and nihilism, back in Kindergarten, when his mother was still alive. He wasn't considered a bad kid, just creative, hyperactive, but also introverted. He attended St. Francis School for Children and always struggled to go to sleep at naptime.

Father Telesco was leading classes. He had finished teaching about the Eucharist and told the children it was naptime. He blessed the kids and tucked them in.

Little Phil was tired, but he wasn't able to calm down enough to take a nap. He liked to think of horror movies and imagine his favorite characters attacking the sleeping students who were mean to him.

He looked at Tony Reezio, who told Phil and his friend Michael Antonio that they were fanooks for each other during arts and crafts. He was about to imagine Freddy Kruger entering his dream and chopping off Tony's wiener, but he caught Father Telesco putting his hand down Tony's pants instead.

Phil gasped. The Father turned his smiling face away from Tony onto Phil's wide-eyed and nauseated stare. The creepy smile left Father's face as he took his hand out of the little Tony's khaki pants.

Father Telesco lifted the same hand up, smelled it, and then made the sign of the cross.

He continued to stare at Phil who was shaking and scared. He walked calmly over to Phil, crouched down over the boy and said, "Your father, Phil, he works construction. He does jobs for the church? Correct?"

Phil nodded yes and forced himself not to cry.

"Yes, little Phil, he does. Do you know, when you lie and say bad things about the Church, God punishes you and your loved ones. You do not want your father to lose his job, do you?"

Phil nodded his head *no*, his eyes glassy and red from trying not to cry.

"I was just checking on Tony. There is no need to cry, my son," Father Telesco told him. "I was making sure the devils were not near his privates. That is where the devil lives. This is a secret of the priests that you must never share. If you tell ... bad things will happen to you, and to your father. God will never stand for someone hurting the Holy Mother Church. Promise me, Phil, swear to God that you won't say a word."

"I promise Father, just don't let God hurt me or my family."

"Swear, Phil. Swear it to God."

"I swear to God."

"Good boy," Father Telesco said. "God is always watching."

Phil never told a soul.

He kept the horror of that day to himself, but his hatred, inward and outward, got stronger year after year, for not telling on Father Telesco. That moment influenced his art but also left him psychologically wounded. Phil always wanted to make up for that day, and having principles and sticking to them was the only way Phil was able to make amends to himself.

Even though it was the right thing for him to take the job from the mafia and break his promise to the Subway owner, a feeling of guilt lingered in his throat along with heartburn from eating so many hot dogs.

Phil was ready to write another poem about how God's love is cum dripping down a Subway sandwich, when a scuzzy *pisan* walked up to the hot stand and said "Hey, what the fuck? Where is Fat Tommy? The gig is tomorrow ... ah shit, Fat Tommy musta got whacked ..."

"I don't know what you're talking about," said Phil. "Do you want a fucking hot dog or not?"

"Yeah, yeah, I got it. You're the new kid taking his place. Ah, *marraone*, Fat Tommy was a good guy. He loved these hot dogs so much. Eh, *fughetabouit*, life goes on, bless that fat fuck's soul. So you are the new camera guy then too?"

"Yeah, I got hired today."

"I'm Pauly, under these circumstances it's not good to meet you, but so it goes."

"I'm Phil, what the fuck you gonna do?"

Pauly nodded his head and said, "Keep on keeping on. Alright, the gig is tomorrow."

"What gig?"

"You don't need to know, just bring your camera. That's why they hired you."

"Ok, but who am I doing the gig for, in case I gotta do research or whatever?"

"You are doing it for three grand, that's who you are doing it for, and you can research my balls. Fucking research, get the fuck out of here."

"Three fucking grand! The Don wasn't bullshitting me!" Phil screamed.

"Keep your fucking voice down, and if you do it right, next time you can get five grand."

"Are you fucking serious?" Phil gasped.

"Hey, listen up. Don't you dare ask for more. I am not getting Jewed by nobody today."

"No, that is fine. I got no complaints."

"Good," Pauly said.

"I'm just grateful. This is a dream true come true. I'll do a good fucking job. I always felt I should get paid good money for my pictures."

"Good, I'll tell PS, he'll be happy to hear that."

"PS?"

"Don't ask so many god damn questions."

"Sorry. Ok. Just excited."

Pauly shook his head and said, "You artists types... *marraone*, you act like fucking broads. Just meet me back here tomorrow. It's a morning shoot. We have to be quick. The spot isn't far."

"I'll bring my camera."

"I'll bring the cash. You get paid after the gig."

8

PHIL CELEBRATED BY EATING THE LAST HOT DOG IN his cart.

He wished he could text or call Missy with the good news, but he didn't believe in cell phones nor was able to afford one. He hated talking to people in general, but besides telling Missy the good news, he wanted to go on to Facebook and tell all those posers that he was going to get paid real money for his art.

Things were finally looking up. He would be finally be out of the doghouse with Missy.

A twenty-something kid with short black hair, holding a plastic bag of hot dog buns and ballpark Franks saw Phil, let out a shocked sighed, and said, "Shit, Fat Tommy is gone. That stupid fuck. I knew he was going to fuck up."

"Yeah, he's ... gone," Phil shrugged.

"Yeah, well I never liked that fat fuck," he said, nodding to Phil. "What up bruh, I'm Johnny Pisstones."

"What the fuck kind of name is that?"

"It's a name of respect, what's your *fanook* name?"

"Phil."

"Like that bald doctor that licks Oprah's asshole. Ha, get the fuck out of here. My shift is on."

"Fine with me," said Phil.

He grabbed his camera but stopped to check out a group of good-looking college students. The guys looked like preppy *meza fanooks*, but the girls were very attractive even the ones with dykey haircuts.

"*Marraone*," Johnny Pisstones said. "Man, these fucking college girls, they are some sweet pieces of *cuse*. It's like their tits are made of marshmallows and candy."

Phil checked out their perky tits and tried to picture their tight assholes, but all he could picture was Missy's perfect ass in his face.

"I'm good with my girl."

"Respect," Johnny Pisstones said. "I'll tell you this, these broads with their Kumbaya Bernie Sanders blowjob bullshit are fucking easy to hustle. Their *meza fanook* boyfriends are even worse. *Stugots*, for a bunch of college kids, they are dumb as fuck. They just like sounding smart talking politics, but they're *fuggazis*. They don't know how the real world works."

Phil shook his head in disgust at the kids and told Johnny, "I hate fucks like that. I wrote a poem about fucks like that..."

Phil began to recite his poem:

> *White college kids*
> *Whose brains have AIDS*
> *Walk the streets*
> *With pre-cum dripping eyes.*
>
> *They think they're savors*
> *But they are Jesus Christ*
> *Bleeding miracle lice*
> *Into our Judas flavored Assholes.*

Johnny Pisstones gave Phil a confused look and said, "For a poet, you're not that much of a *mezza fanook*, but you're one weird fuck. You might need to get some good college pussy to get your head straight. Your girl don't have to know. Just find a little rich girl and make her you *goomah*."

Phil was turned on by the thought of a licking a college girl's asshole, but at the end of the day the only girl's asshole he wanted to lick was Missy's.

"Nah, like I said, I got a great girl," Phil said and walked to his bus stop.

Phil rode the bus home wondering what it would feel like to get paid so much money for his photography. He believed he deserved monetary success but he never felt it would ever come to him. The only thing that made this belief bearable was venting about it on Facebook, and escaping his surroundings in horror movies.

He leaned back in his seat and looked out the window. He thought about how the streets of Jersey were getting more fucked up each year. Phil tried to think of better times, but Jersey had always been a dysfunctional shithole. The only time he liked living in Jersey was when his mom was alive. He missed going home after pre-school to see her, but today he dreaded going home and seeing Missy and his father.

Phil opened the bus window and took out a cigarette. He lit it, took a big drag, and he figured it all balanced out in the end.

The bus stopped to pick up passengers by a Catholic Church, and Phil stuck his head out the window and exhaled.

He snuck a couple more drags, but heard a familiar voice screech at him, "Philip LoPresti. Philip is that you?"

Philip coughed and cringed. He remembered that voice and still had nightmares of it.

It was the voice of Nun Mahoney.

He flicked away the half-smoked cigarette out the window, turned around, and saw Nun Mahoney standing in the isle, her wrinkled face scowling and arms folded with disapproval. Behind her were two younger nuns.

"Excuse me, sisters," Nun Mahoney said. "I know this cretin. I taught him from Kindergarten to grade school. He liked to smoke on the school bus in grade school too. I see not much has changed."

The two sisters nodded and made the sign of the cross. They grabbed a seat up front, but Sister Mahoney joined Phil in the back. She sat to his right, looked forward, and said, "I saw your name in the paper. I wasn't surprised. Your art is a crime against God."

"So is child molestation."

She turned her head at him and stared with anger. "How dare you, Philip. Those falsities are antichrist attacks of the Jewish Media. I tried to help you see the love of Christ, but you stole the Christ Died For Our Sins Doll. Like a deviant, you stole used tampons from the girls' bathroom room and put the feminine products in doll Jesus's hands. It was disgusting! I see you're still doing the same blasphemous satanic garbage."

"It was stigmata through virgin blood! It was art!"

The nun slapped Philip in the face just like she used to when he acted up in fourth grade. Phil felt like that scared child again, and part him wanted to cry, but the other part of him just wanted to call her cunt.

He kept quiet and rubbed his cheek.

"You're not 'artistic' Phil. You're a loser. You always will be."

Phil pulled the lever to get off the bus and walk the rest of the way home. He forced himself to stand up to her and said, "I might be a loser but you're a liar. I know you protected Father Telesco and knew about the kids he fondled."

"I did not."

"You did, and one day I'll be a famous photographer and poet and I'll tell on YOU FUCKS."

"Ha, that's a laugh. You failed English."

"That's because you had me write about that gay fucking bible."

"The Bible is not gay!"

"Maybe not, but Father Telesco was for little boys."

The Nun gritted her teeth and whispered, "Fuck you, LoPresti. Fuck you, you little shit."

The bus came to a stop and Phil said, "I see you haven't changed either Nun Mahoney," and walked off the bus.

Phil walked the rest of the way home seething with anger and regret.

The nun's words had stung and stirred up a deep resentment that clung to him since he was child.

He arrived home and saw his dad's car parked in the driveway. Phil looked at the back bumper with bumper stickers *Pisan Pride* with an Italian flag and *Honk if Your Sons A Disappointment Too.*

Phil shook his head and spit at the car.

When he was a kid, the only thing more traumatic than the nuns was when his father got drunk. Mr. LoPresti's drinking got worse after Phil's mother died. He was a mean drunk. It got so bad that Phil's dad went back to Church. He sobered up and didn't even drink the Church wine.

Phil sighed and walked to his front door, knowing Missy wouldn't be home for dinner for another hour. He would just be stuck with his dad.

He opened the door and saw his dad sitting in the living room. Mr. LoPresti looked up from reading the South Jersey Paper and said, "Well, what was the verdict? Whatever it is, I'm not paying it."

"They found me guilty but ..."

"But nothing, *marraone! Bafangool, stugots*! You better not skip town and leave me and Missy with the bill."

"Let me finish..."

"*Fughetabouit*, you are finished."

"I'm not. I got a job."

"What putting diapers on piss clams?"

"No, I am going to make real money. Taking pictures for rich Italian businessmen."

"So you're gonna do bullshit for the mob?"

Phil stayed quiet and shrugged his shoulders to answer his father.

"I told you to stay away from those crooked guineas. They are bad for our people. Goddamn it, Philip. You get your stupidity and carelessness from your mother."

"Leave her out of this, and it is still a big time gig. I am getting paid to real photography. I'm finally making it! I am going to be a working photographer. I'll be able to pay the fine, not go to jail, and get compensated finally for my brilliance!"

"Brilliant, ha, *fughetabouit. Bafangool*, thinking you're a big shot photographer cause you got one gig. Get a 100 of those and then we'll talk, and have those other 99 not be for the fucking mob. You're playing with fire Phil. Playing with fire."

"You don't get it, pops. We should be celebrating, not arguing! My art is finally going to make some money."

"Yeah, your *art*. It's because of your so called *art* that you are in this situation, killing old ladies with your filth. What a fucking disgrace."

"My art shows the disgrace of existence."

"Hey watch it, that's blasphemy right there. Show some respect to God and the gift of life."

"The only gift is death! God is dead!"

"Go to your room, I don't want to hear this Marilyn Manson *fanook* bullshit."

"It's my house!"

"It's Missy's, she pays the rent and I'm still you father. Go to your fucking room!"

"Fine!"

9

Phil laid down in his bed and opened his laptop.

He logged into Facebook and saw the same old writer friends sharing book reviews their friends wrote. They were also tagging each other about the awesome interviews they gave each other, and sharing memes that made the photographer in him wish for human genocide or a *memeocide*.

All these so-called artists made Phil want to puke.

What a bunch of posers, he thought, *they never made art so powerful it would give an old lady a heart attack. Safe, self-congratulatory, artistic miscarriages. Fucking garbage.*

Phil shook his head in usual disgust at what he saw on Facebook.

He was busting his ass to be compensated as a real artist, that it lead him to work for the mafia and sell hot dogs for them, but he couldn't even get an interview from fellow writers because he didn't want to kiss ass.

The term *literary citizenship* just meant one big circle jerk of mediocrity. There were no more Bukowski's, Plath's, or Baudelaire's, just a bunch of bullshitters who liked the label *author*, but would be better off working at a bank or as a guidance counselor.

Everything and everyone was awful.

Phil logged onto Facebook to feel better and less alone, but every time, he only felt worse.

Filled with rage and alienation, Phil posted on his wall, "YOU ARE ALL PATHETIC POSERS! FACEBOOK SHOULD BE CALLED FACIAL GROUP! ALL YOU DO IS CUM ON EACH OTHER'S FACES AND LICK IT OFF. NONE OF YOU ARE MAKING REAL ART AND NONE OF YOU ARE EVEN GETTING PAID. IT'S ONE BIG CIRCLE JERK, AND IF YOU ARE MAKING MONEY IT'S CRAP LIKE CHRISTOPH PAUL WRITES WITH DINOSAURS CUMMING ON D-LIST ACTORS. EVERY WRITER ON FACEBOOK IS EITHER MEDIOCRE, UNTALENTED, OR A HACK LIKE CHRISTOPH (WHO IS MY FRIEND, BUT HE IS STILL A HACK AND REPRE-SENTS THE DEATH OF LITERATURE—NO OFFENSE CHRISTOPH, YOU GREEDY FUCKING JEW FUCK!!!) BUT GUESS WHAT YOU FUCKS?!?! I HAVE A REAL GIG! A FUCKING PAYING GIG! A RICH FUCK SEES THE GENUIS IN MY PHOTOGRAPHY AND HIRED ME. I'M ALSO DOING RESEARCH ABOUT SELLING HOT DOGS AND MY NEXT POETRY BOOK WILL BE ABOUT THE WORKING MAN OF JERSEY. I HAVE TO WORK NOT LIKE YOU FUCKS IN BROOKLYN AND PORTLAND DOING YOUR POT YOGA AND EATING YOUR VOODOO DONUTS. NO! I MAKE REAL ART IN THE REAL WORLD! AND AS YOU SAW, I ACTUALLY AFFECT THE REAL WORLD. PEOPLE DIE WITNESSING MY ART! I AM A REAL ARTIST AND I DON'T SPEND MY TIME JERKING OFF OTHER SHITTY WRITERS. SO WHILE YOU GO WRITE AND SELF-PUBLISH EACH OTHERS SHITTY TALKING PENIS BOOKS, I'LL BE SELLING HOT DOGS AND MAKING MONEY OFF MY PHOTOGRAPHY. I NEED THE MONEY BECAUSE MY ART IS SO POWERFUL AND BRILLIANT IT KILLED AN OLD LADY AND

MADE HER SHIT HER PANTS. SOME OF YOU ARE CONDEMNING ME FOR THIS, BUT YOU ARE JUST MEDIOCRE PUSSIES. REAL ART CAN KILLLLLLL! SO KEEPING MAKING SHIT ART, I'LL GO MAKE MONEY MAKING PEOPLE SHIT IN THEIR PANTS, YOU TALENTLESS FUCKS!!!!!"

Phil pressed entered and waited to see how many *likes* he'd get or comments and congratulations about his new job, but only Christoph Paul wrote, "Congrats Phil! I respect your honesty."

That fucking dickhead, thought Phil.

He waited for at least a few likes but he only saw his *friends-list* going down.

"Fucking pussies," he said out loud to himself, "Real artists want to hear the truth... they like actually hearing ..." Phil stopped talking to himself, hearing a car pulling into the drive-way. He figured Missy must have gotten a ride.

He dreaded going back out there with his dad.

Even with the great photography gig and the new job, Phil felt a wave of loneliness come over him. There was no one to share the good and bad news with, who wouldn't judge him.

He was alone.

Phil looked back at his friends list dropping and felt such disdain because he knew a lot of those writers on Facebook had all the things he wished he received in life: the support of good friends and family.

He stayed in his room and put on his favorite album by *Swans, The Great Annihilator*.

Phil tried to lose himself in the *Swans* album. The band always helped him feel a little better and the album was inspiring him to attempt a poem about futility of life. He started writing out lines but heard a knock on the door.

"What? I'm writing poetry. Nothing is an important as that."

"Ay, yah, Phil," said Mr. LoPresti. "Missy is here and she is with some, um, neighborhood guys … you need to come out here right now, Phil!"

Thoughts of what would be the third line left Phil.

Worry came to him instead.

He opened his door and saw the Martino Family sitting at the table with Missy, looking scared.

"Hey, *pisan*," said Dean Martino. "I didn't know you were Tom LoPresti's kid. I've known yours pops for long time, he's good guy from the neighborhood. He always minds his business and acts respectful. Not like you kid. Ha! I'm just busting your balls. I just met your girl, Missy. Lovely girl. We had a nice talk. I gave her a ride home, but if you do good for us, Phil, you'll be able to buy her a car in no time."

Phil was not okay with the Martino Family picking up Missy. He didn't want her involved in any of this. He saw his father putting on a fake face of respect, but Missy was really struggling to hide her feelings.

No matter how many fuck ups, she always loved him and found a way to make things work out. Phil wondered if he had finally gone too far.

He forced himself to nod his head to show gratitude and resect. "Ugh, yeah. Thanks for giving her a ride home, Mr. Martino."

Dean Martino smiled. "Of course. I take care of my guys. Let's go outside for a little bit. Talk about work tomorrow."

"Okay Mr. Martino."

"Call me Dean, kid."

Phil followed him and the Mafiosos out his front door to their Cadillacs parked to the side of Mr. LoPresti's Trans Am.

Boss Martino took out a cigarette. Phil lit up Dean Martino's cigarette and then lit up his own. Martino took a drag and said, "We know about the Paki's messing with you, don't worry about them. They'll pay. Those fucking camel jockeys and their shit sandwiches, *marraone*. But no worries, fughetabouit. The longer they wait to pay, the more hot dog stands we'll put up."

"That is okay. I like selling hot dogs."

The guys laughed and Dean Martino said, "Philip we didn't just give you this job to sell hot dogs. We know who you are. We read the paper. We know you're some artsy kook from the neighborhood, but that is what this job needs. A *pisan* who is a real *mezza fanook*, but can still be trusted to take some good pictures."

"I'm grateful, Dean Martino. I'll do a good job, I promise, whatever it is."

"I know you will, or else..."

The other *pisans* laughed and Martino said, "You will do just fine kid. You just got to do the gig tomorrow. It's just taking pictures of the weird stuff, that is where are money is now. The FEDS cracked down on us since the fucking 90's, so the mullions took the drugs and whores, the kikes took over money laundering, gambling, and Hollywood, and now the Pakis are taking all the fast food places and not giving us tribute. Fucking *stu gotz*, sometimes I think we should go back to Italy. But we found some business and we are making good. If you do good with it, you can make damn good money with us too."

"I need the money."

"Good, we'll give it to you, just do the work."

"Who am I working with tomorrow?"

"Hey don't ask so many fucking questions."

"Sorry."

"He's my son, so be good to him. He's a writer and photographer, and weird *mezza fanook* fuck like you. You just do what he says. You do a good job, you get paid. You do a bad job we'll pay you and you girlfriend another visit. You don't want that," Martino said and rounded up his crew to get going.

Phil walked back into his house.

His father stood up and said, "I don't want any part of this Phil. You and Missy are on your own."

Mr. LoPresti walked right out of the house and slammed the door behind him.

"Hey dad, wait!" Phil yelled.

But Phil's dad didn't want to hear anymore. He started his car and drove right off.

"Fine. I'll make more money than you, YOU DRY DRUNK FUCK!" Phil screamed at the car that was already a block away.

He turned around back toward the table and saw Missy sitting in the same spot smoking a cigarette. She said nothing. She smoked and looked down at the floor.

Phil knew he had really fucked up.

"I was going to tell you Missy."

"Tell me what?"

"That the trial went bad, but that I got a good job afterwards. I took initiative like you always bitch at me to do."

"Working for the mafia!? And doing god knows what," she said and shook her head in disgust.

"I'm their photographer and a hot dog salesman. I'm not whacking anybody or doing crimes. I will finally get paid for my art."

"They are criminals, Phil!" Missy screamed back, "and they scared the shit out me, picking me up like that. I thought they were going to kill me. And it's not a job, Phil, you have to do whatever they want you to do or they'll kill you ... *and me.*"

Phil felt horrible. He never feared death, but the one person he never wanted to hurt was Missy.

He lit up a cigarette, exhaled with frustration, and said, "I didn't know they'd get you involved."

Phil then thought of all the fuck ups he had put Missy through. It always looked like he was screwed, but Missy would forgive him and find a solution. Phil worried this time he might have gone too far and said, "I'll just do the gig and then I'll quit and try to..."

Phil stopped. He wasn't sure if they'd even let him quit, or what he would do after that. There were no good jobs and if he screwed up working this one, it wouldn't just be him paying the price.

Missy looked up to him and caressed his face. "I love you, you god damn asshole. That is the only reason why I stay with you, but I don't know how we will get through this one."

Phil didn't know either but tried to point out the good. "At least I'm getting paid for photography, and I'm getting a lot. You said to have goals. Well, I'm finally hitting one."

"You don't even know what you're shooting."

"Who cares, it's three grand."

"I care. And I'm scared. I'm really scared, Phil."

"I hear ya. I am too." Phil grabbed her hand and said, "Come to bed with me. I want to hold you. It's going to be hard for me to get to sleep, I got to get up early to do this ... thing."

Missy let go of Phil's hand and said, "I want be alone right now and just process what is happening."

Phil nodded that he understood. He walked over to the couch and opened up his laptop see if anyone had liked his Facebook status.

PART 3

10

———

PHIL HAD TO ADMIT THAT HOT DOGS SMELLED THE BEST IN the morning.

By the afternoon, the fumes and heat would mix in with the burnt meat and it smelled like charred brothel mattresses, but in the morning they smelled a little like the breakfast sausages his mom used to make.

He stood by his cart, smoking a cigarette. There were no customers wanting hot dogs this early. He kept his eyes out for the Subway Pakistani men, but the streets were desolate. There were no cars parked nearby.

Phil tossed his cigarette and ate another hot dog.

He was upset that Missy never joined him for bed. He had woken up from a nightmare, went to the kitchen to get a snack and found her passed out with the house phone near her head.

There were dried tears on her face and Phil felt even worse. He gave her a kiss, but he wasn't able to fall back to sleep after seeing her like that.

Even the idea of making real money by taking photographs didn't take away the shitty feeling of making Missy so upset.

He decided that if God was alive He was a sadistic cunt-rag.

Phil grabbed a pen from his pocket to write a poem to exorcise his feelings.

> *God pre-came*
> *and the angels*
> *took a shit.*
>
> *The cum mixed*
> *with angel feces*
> *and man was born.*
>
> *For God hated the world*
> *that he gave man mouths*
> *and with them we eat*
>
> *hot dogs*
> *hoping to die ...*

Phil didn't know how to finish the poem.

He thought it needed one more line. He tried to find the rhythm and perfect phrase to signify the meaninglessness and hell of existence but a voice said, "Hey mister, can I get a hotdog. My mom's a cunt and didn't give me any breakfast."

Phil looked up to see a redhead kid in a catholic school uniform. He grabbed the kid a hot dog, handed it to him, and said, "You shouldn't call your mom that. Mine is now a corpse. You should know that every woman is a cunt except your mom, Sylvia Plath, and your girlfriend."

"Whatever. Who is Sylvia Plath?"

"She's a poet who hated everyone and everything and expressed in the most beautiful way possible."

"I hate everyone, but I think poetry is gay."

"Get the fuck out of here, you little fuck. Poetry isn't gay, being a fucking ginger is gay."

"Whatever, asshole ... let me get some mustard, first."

"Fine, but what is really gay is that school of yours. Don't trust the priests or the nuns. They are evil!"

"Yeah, I hate the priests."

"You're a smart kid. Stay in school, but be careful."

"I guess so," the kid said and finished putting mustard on his hot dog. "Were you bad in school? Is that why you sell hot dogs?"

"The world is bad, and when you're good, the world fucks you in the ass."

The boy looked upset and then ran away.

"Hey, what the fuck did I say? You need to pay me YOU FUCK!" Phil screamed, but it was too late, the boy was gone.

For a second Phil was tempted to chase after him, but he saw Pauly walking toward his hot dog stand.

He smiled at Phil and said, "Yo, make me a fucking hot dog and then follow me. We are heading to the photo shoot."

Phil followed the Mafioso.

After they walked eight blocks, Phil was ready to light up another cigarette, but Pauly said, "Ok kid, we're here, put the smokes away."

Phil looked up and saw a Catholic Church with the sign: *Our Lady of Lords Primary Charter School and Church.*

He placed his cigarette back in his pack and said, "A fucking church? And what the fuck kind of school is this?"

"It's a charter school for poor and foreigner kids. What the fuck does it matter?"

"I don't know. I just fucking hate Catholic Churches. I think they should all be burnt down."

"Hey, nobody asked your goddamn opinion. You take that devil shit somewhere else. Just do your fucking job. You are hired to take photos for the boss's son. He does his art here."

"What?" Phil said and looked confused. "Here?"

"What did I tell ya, you fucking *stu gotz,* no questions! Just go inside and do your fucking job. I'll come back in an hour and you'll get paid."

"OK, OK. I got it."

"Good. You got your camera ready?"

"Of course."

"Alright. Good. And no poetry or *fanook* bullshit. You keep your mouth shut and you take whatever pictures he wants."

"Yeah, yeah. I got it."

Pauly nodded and signaled for Phil to walk through the Church doors.

Phil opened a heavy door that slowly shut behind him.

The church was empty, but he heard the sound of two men. He walked toward the hallway to the right of the large cross with a bleeding Christ. He saw a room with dark windows, with children's drawings of different Saints, and it said 'Jesus's Classroom' in gold letters upon the door. Phil walked to it and peaked through the small window on top of the door. Inside, there were sleeping children, a priest, and a strange dark haired man that Phil could have sworn he had seen before.

Phil opened the door and the young priest said, "Welcome, we are pleased to see you. We must hurry. Get your camera ready for Mr. Sotos."

The dark haired man was staring at the children and didn't even bother saying hello to Phil.

Phil gave the man a closer look and recognized him.

He was the transgressive author, Peter Sotos, who got in trouble for pornography and lewd images in his magazines. Phil always forgot to look up what the images were, but he respected anyone who managed to get censored. This photography gig was turning out better than he imagined.

"Whoa, I know you," Phil told Peter Sotos. "You are an author and photographer too, I didn't know you're Dean Martino's kid."

Sotos kept his gaze fixed upon the sleeping children and said, "It's a pen name. Father Cardinal, have the boy here sign the contract and then we can make some real art."

"Cool," Phil said with excitement, "This is an honor. People say you're hardcore."

"Oh yes, we shall capture the innocence that our society has taken way," Peter Sotos said, looking solemnly at the children.

Phil watched the Priest place a sleeping boy on the communion table.

Phil recognized the kid. It was the same little red-headed boy he'd sold the hot dog to earlier that day.

The Priest placed the redheaded child next to the sacraments and said, "I am ready. What I will do is better than God."

"Wow, a blasphemous priest," said Phil, smiling. "This is cool as fuck. I like that you're using a ginger, it shows how we are all soulless."

"Silence," instructed Peter Sotos. "Just take the pictures. Alright Father Cardinal, we are doing a sacrament; we are going to feel the love that the Greeks knew that made them be at one with Dionysus."

"Yes Sir, Mr. Sotos."

"Drink the wine, that is not Christ, but of every child's tear of innocence," said Sotos.

"Yes, sir," said the Priest, guzzling the wine.

"Feel the communion of youth and then place it in your mouth," Sotos ordered. "Photoman you smell like hotdog puke. I will forgive you for coming to our sacred place smelling so putrid as long as you take excellent pictures."

Phil nodded and got his camera ready.

He started taking the pictures of the Priest getting closer to the boy.

Phil went from being excited by the blasphemy to feeling uncomfortable and nauseous watching the Priest hover over the boy.

He dropped his camera when he saw the Priest unzip the red-headed boy's pants. It bounced on his shoe onto the floor.

"Fuck," said Phil, ducking down and picking up the camera.

He took a few practice shots of the floor and saw it was ok.

"Get up and shoot you fool, the magic is starting," Peter Sotos ordered.

Phil pointed the camera again at the priest and the boy, but dropped it again seeing the priest moving toward the young boy's genitals. Phil had seen some terrible things in his life but this topped it all.

Phil was horrified, disgusted, and wanted to kill.

He glanced around at the other children. He saw a brown skinned boy who looked Pakistani, with tears streaming down his face.

The boy mouthed silently to Phil, "Help."

"Hey!" barked Sotos, "Take the goddamn picture or I'll get my father after you. You'll be dead in an hour."

"Ooh, yes," The priest said, ready to put the boy's penis in his mouth. "The communion is here."

Phil ran up to priest and kicked him hard in the balls.

The priest dropped to the floor into the fetal position. A

nauseous yelped drooled out of his lips, as he tried to lift himself up on the edge of the classroom blackboard, but Phil kicked him again. The priest's head slammed against the hard metal rim of the blackboard. Blood gushed from the back of his head and the white chalk dust turned red.

"Oh shit. Fuck me!" Peter Sotos ran, with Phil following close behind.

11

Peter Sotos ran into the confession booth and locked the door.

Phil tried to open it but it wouldn't budge. He kicked at the door and heard Sotos on his cellphone. "Dad! Come quick. The photographer, he attacked the priest and he's trying to do me in next. Come now, please! He's got me trapped, dad! Come whack this philistine!"

"Get off the phone YOU FUCK!!!" said Phil, entering the priest's booth.

"You better run," sputtered Sotos through the confession screen. "You are so fucked. So dead. The whole Martino Family is coming for you right now."

"Fuck you, I don't give a fuck!" screamed Phil. "I fucking hate child molesters more than anything! Even more than *Nightbreed*!"

"I love *Nightbreed*! It's my favorite movie," Sotos shot back. "YOU SICK FUCK!"

Phil still didn't believe in God, but he felt a calling to stop Peter Sotos. He started ripping out pages of a Bible and stuffing them through the confession divider.

"What are you doing? My dad will be here so soon. You're so fucking dead! Stop! I'm artist, just like you."

"You're not an artist, you're a fucking deviant pedo FUCK," Phil screamed, lighting all the Bible pages on fire.

Before Sotos could yell at Phil to stop, Phil blew on the flame and it went right at Peter Sotos' face. The gel in his hair caught fire along with his beard. Sotos' whole head went up in flames like he was the comic book character Ghostrider.

Phil stepped out of the confession booth and Pete Sotos screamed and banged against the walls. "HELP ME! HELP! HEEEELLLLL..."

"That is where you're going YOU FUCK!" Phil said but decided that Sotos deserved to be raped in prison. Death was too merciful a fate for this fuck. He left the booth and picked up the small fountain holding the communion water. He brought it back the booth and threw the holy water onto Sotos' burning face.

Smoke spread throughout the Church. The mobster's son wasn't dead, but the majority of his face was already burnt off.

Phil walked out of the booth and saw the Pakistani kid.

"Are you an angel sent by Allah to protect the children?"

Phil wanted to tell the kid there was no god and the whole world was fucked and pointless, but he said, "Yeah. I'm an angel sent to give justice for the children."

"Petey boy! Petey boy! I'm coming!" a voice outside the locked church door screamed.

Someone fired a gun. The lock was shot off lock and the door burst open.

"Go and hide with the order boys," Phil told the boy. "I'll deal with these FUCKS."

"Angels don't curse," the boy said.

"Yeah, we fucking do. Go now!"

12

THE MOBSTERS BARGED IN WITH THEIR GUNS.

Out of respect, they made the sign of the cross with their pistols and then pointed them at Phil.

"Where is my fucking son?" demanded Dean Martino.

Phil was too scared to speak.

Fuck, he thought himself, *I'm going to die in a god damn church, not smothered to death by Missy sitting on my face like I always wanted.*

The boss placed his gun against Phil's temple. "Don't make me ask twice."

"In the confession booth ... I burned his fucking face off."

The mob boss choked back a sob and said, "I thought about killing him so many times. But you can't kill blood. I got into the kiddy porn business to keep us afloat and make my son's sin at least have some fucking value ..."

"Child molesters deserve to be fucking tortured!" screamed Phil.

"Shut the fuck up!" yelled Dean Martino. He kept his gun pointed at Phil but turned to his men and ordered, "Get me my kid's body, we'll get him to Dr. Schino, and we'll bury this fuck in the woods. Don't worry Philly boy, we are going to get your girl-friend too. You two can be buried together."

Phil still felt no fear of death. It always sounded like a good deal, but he couldn't stomach the idea of Missy dying because of him and said, "You can fucking whack me right now, but leave Missy the fuck alone. She is the best girl. She is a saint. You're gonna kill a fucking saint. Just take me instead, fucking kill me right here, just don't touch Missy."

"She might be a saint, but if she is stupid enough to be with you, she is stupid enough to get fucking whacked."

"What the fuck! I thought the Mafia was about honor and shit. Working with child molesters and killing girlfriends. That is some fucking *fuggazi* bullshit."

"Hey, you don't know shit, kid. That was before the *mulli*, spics, kikes, Coleslaws, and now the sand *mulli* terrorists started eating all the pie. We'd die if we lived with honor."

"What the fuck is a coleslaw?" Phil questioned trying to buy time.

"The fucking Russians."

"I hate the Russians," Phil said. "You should hire me. I could go kill all the Russians. I pay the debt that way. I'll be your mafia assassin slave."

"My guys can handle the fucking Russians. Stop stalling us."

"Fine. Please, please use some honor, that old-school Italian honor, and don't hurt Missy. Please."

"You should have been like your old man. He gets it. He understands respect, that's why we will let him live. But you and her, that will be my justice."

"Fuck, come on. Just take me. Please I'll do anything."

Dean Martino laughed and said, "Ha, fucking poets. So dramatic. How bout this, you tell me a poem right now and if it's great I'll spare your girlfriend."

"You serious?"

"No, I fucking hate poetry. It's for *fanooks*. But go ahead say your poem. I'll give the courtesy of some final words, then I kill you and go kill your girlfriend."

"Missy!" Phil called out like she could hear him. "This poem is for you. I am so sorry."

"These are you last words, but we will share it to Missy before we kill her too."

13

———

Phil closed his eyes and begged a universe that had no meaning or purpose to please let Missy live.

Then he heard a loud sound.

He assumed it was a gun, and accepted death.

But death did not come.

"What the fuck, just kill me!" Phil screamed with his eyes still shut.

"Drop your weapons now! Do it! Get on the ground!" Phil heard another voice scream.

He opened his eyes and saw a group of police officers pointing their guns at Dean Martino and the Mafiosos who were carrying Peter Soto's charred and unconscious body.

The men dropped Soto's body and held up their hands.

"This kid is a murderer and pedophile," said Dean Martino. "He attacked my son, the priest, and was going to fuck the kids. He's crazed. This was self-defense, arrest this fucking pervert."

"No," a young voice said from behind the pews. "That boy is no boy, he is angel who saved me. He is hero. He saved all of us from great sin."

The little Pakistani boy stood up and pointed his hand at the mobsters. "They are the bad ones. The angel boy is good, for all angels are good, Inshallah."

"Oh shit there is a kid," said the head police officer.

Two cops ran to the boy. "You okay, kid? Did they do anything to you?" they asked, kneeling down.

The Pakistani boy was shaking and said, "The burnt man and priest did bad things to my friend. The angel who curses, he saved us. He is hero and an angel. Angels can do no wrong, because they come from God, Allah Hu Akbar."

"Yeah," Phil said. "I am a god damn angel and a hero."

"The kid is in shock, get him help," said the lead police officer. "And get these scumbags cuffed and read them their rights. The Martino Family will be charged for child pornography."

"The fucking poet did it. We are innocent!" Dean Martino protested while the cops handcuffed him and his whole crew.

"Yeah, tell it to the judge. The prosecutor has a RICO case and we got a witness."

"A sand *mulli* child? Ha, good luck." Dead Martino said, as he was being escorted out in cuffs.

"It's Pakistani YOU RACIST FUCK!" said LoPresti.

"Read them their rights and get the boy some counseling, and get his father here," the head policeman said, "And bring in a medic for the priest and that Ghostface looking pedo."

Phil took out a cigarette and lit up. He took a nice long drag and said, "I still hate the police. I think you all are fascists pigs, but thanks ... for you know ... saving me. I didn't care about dying, but they threatened to kill my girlfriend and she is one of the few people who deserve to live, you know, besides these kids."

The policeman nodded with a confused face and said, "Son, it was your girlfriend Missy that gave us the tip last night. She warned us that you were trying to make a citizen's arrest on the mob and needed protection. She said that we should follow behind you. Thank God we did. We've been trying to bust this crew for decades. Your girlfriend's tip enabled us to get a warrant and your immunity. She is a great girl. You and your girlfriend, you're freaking heroes."

Phil took another drag and said, "Fucking Missy, she's a god damn saint."

"Son," the head police said. "I understand you must be feeling a lot of things, but please don't curse in the Church."

"Sorry, this just got me all fuuu ... I mean .... yeah."

"It's alright, we followed you from the hot dog stand. We got the guy who took you too. When we saw Dean Martino going into the Church we followed him inside. I just wish we followed you sooner. You did a great work here, going undercover like this was brave."

"I hate child molesters with all my heart. I actually wrote a poem about the pedos that show up on that Chris Hansen show in my chapbook *Sodomize Molesters and Feed Them to Satanic Ants*. I think it is my best book besides *I Am Suicide*."

"That is um ... some righteous anger there, son. And yes, you are a true American hero..." the cop stopped as the news vans drove up. "It angers me to even think about what those scumbags were doing with these kids."

Phil nodded and looked out the widow. He saw more news vans than cop cars. "What is all this?"

"The news, kid. They will want to speak to you, and you'll have to go to court, but you'll be innocent. We got a witness and we aren't letting these guys get off. Don't worry, we are going to make sure justice is served."

Phil took another drag. "Damn, I still got to pay the court the money, I owe to that old ladies' family. Shit, I got to go to court twice now."

"Oh yeah, you're the kid from the paper. I thought I recognized you. Crazy week for you, kid."

"Yeah, it was. And I still need to make some money to pay the funeral. Hey officer, do I get a reward for doing a good thing for the community?"

The cop shook his head no and said, "No son, but you did a great deed for your community, and that is the best reward."

14

A PRESS CONFERENCE WAS SET UP IN FRONT OF OUR LADY of Lords Church. Phil stood with the cops as the local news stations asked the Police Chef questions. Phil could see the national news was starting to show up as well.

He stood beside them, feeling pride and anxiety, while smoking a cigarette. It was a nice and new feeling for Phil to feel pleased and proud of himself. He was proud of himself for burning off Peter Sotos' face and stopping the mafia child porn ring, but he was already worrying about how to get the money to pay his legal bills.

He was sick of disappointing Missy and he was scared of going to jail. Especially now, knowing the mob would be there. He was also sick of ending up in situations where Missy had to bail him out. He was sick of his art not selling as well as *The Premature Penis Ejaculators vs. The Alien Vaginas From Pluto Part 3*.

Most of all, he was sick of feeling so sick of life.

Phil took his last drag and heard the Police chief say, "We used the tip of a citizen, and we followed this brave young man to the church. He went undercover as a hot dog salesman and led us to this horrendous crime. Let's give him a round of applause."

The crowd cheered and the police chief continued, "Philip LoPresti, hero of New Jersey, tell these good folks the inspiration and bravery behind your courageous act."

The crowd clapped and cheered and Phil felt uncomfortable with so much praise and goodwill.

He lit up another cigarette and walked up to the podium.

The police chief smiled at him and shook his hand. Phil wasn't able to smile but he nodded and took another drag.

He adjusted his microphone and looked out into the crowd. He saw a media who didn't care about those kids and the people who wanted to feel a part of his act of heroism, cheering and finding meaning, not in themselves, but in his good deed. He kept the cigarette in his mouth and starred. Deep down he always wanted to be loved by society, and they were finally giving him what he secretly craved but it felt more hollow than the Church standing behind him.

The whole crowd disgusted him and he found them as pathetic as the all the wannabe writers online.

"Alright, shut up," said Phil.

He felt like he was about to make one of his infamous misanthropic Facebook posts, except this would actually be on the national news. *Fuck it*, Phil thought. *Bukowski and Baudelaire speak from the heart, not from their taint.*

He smiled, took another drag and said, "Alright, you *fuggazis*. I'm going to say my piece. Listen or not, I don't give shit. The truth is, is I'm not a fucking hero. I am just a good poet, and if I don't die in twenty years, maybe I'll be great. I'm a photographer too. I just was at the right place at the right time to catch and stop some fucked up shit. It was horrible. But I enjoyed burning off Peter Sotos' face, because that is what should happen to child rapists. Experiencing that and almost getting killed by the Mafia helps you see the real truth. I'm looking out into the audience seeing your admiration turn to disdain like I might as well be a fucking pedo like Peter Sotos or Jared and I see you're all full of shit. You all think the church behind this is a good place. FUCK CHURCHES! They should all be burned down, because they give pedos room and board, food, and fresh kids to fondle. But YOU FUCKS lick the Pope's asshole and let them live tax free, while poor fucks like me have to sell hot dogs and bring down the mafia and still owe your stupid philistine asses money, because you are too weak and fucking stupid to appreciate real fucking art! I am an artist and have been fighting to share the horrors of life but none of you give a fuck. The world doesn't care about art and if you did you wouldn't have these kids be with these sick Catholic fucks, who might grow up to be pedos too ..." the booing started, the policeman chief was shocked, but Phil kept going. "Go ahead and boo! Boos are claps for the truth. You are all hypocrites and full of shit. I wrote a chapbook about murdering pedophiles but I didn't get a fucking parade. No one gave a shit. I just did the right thing, none of you do the right thing, cause YOU FUCKS are always wrong. The shit that happened is because you fear sex and violence in art and entertainment, but you let pedos watch your fucking kids. Yeah, go ahead and boo. Boo the fucking hero, even Jesus was crucified by YOU FUCKS. The truth is, art and all gods are dead, and you all worship bullshit. I am giving you the truth and you don't want it! Well, I don't want your fickle and fuckhead love either! All I need is Missy and my few fans. The rest of you FUCKS can fuck off!"

People started to throw things at the stage and the cop took the microphone away from Phil and said, "Forgive the boy, he probably has PSTD."

Phil flicked off the crowd but took his finger down when he saw Missy in the crowd looking furious.

15

The crowd dispersed and all the reporters left Phil to himself. The only person who stayed and approached him was a very pissed off Missy.

She wanted to curse him out, but she hugged him instead. She held him tight and kissed him.

Phil was surprised and said, "You're not mad?"

Missy slapped him hard across the face. "I'm mad that I'm in love with a guy who was almost got killed by the mafia and cursed out all of America."

"Who cares about that, Missy, I knocked out a priest and burnt a pedophile's face off. It was brutal and righteous justice. I am a fucking a hero."

Missy rolled her eyes. "Two wrongs don't make a right."

"So you're proud of me?"

"I don't know Phil, all I know is I've been worried sick for the last twelve hours, and I'm sick of having to avert disasters you keep getting yourself into. You are alive cause I alerted the police."

"That was fucking dumb, Missy."

"No it wasn't, Phil. You're alive because I did."

"So that was what you were doing last night?"

"Yeah. I couldn't sleep. I stayed up trying to figure out a solution... I even Googled what to do and this was the best answer I could come up with. I learned to alert the police if you were trying to make a citizen's arrest. They'd give you immunity for any crime. I didn't want you to go to jail and I especially didn't want you to die."

"It worked, but I'm actually still going to fucking jail."

"Yeah, you are, because you treated your media interview like it was a goddamn Facebook post! People could have maybe given you money, a job, or a reward if you just acted decently. Who knows, maybe you could have gotten a book deal. Anything, but you did what you always do. Only you, Phil, could do a good act and still end up as hated as that Pharma Bro guy."

"Fuck that, I tell the fucking truth. A real artist does."

"No, a real asshole does."

"IT'S THE SAME FUCKING THING!"

"Well, Mr. Truth Teller you can now speak the truth in jail or have us go into even worse debt, because no one is going to be hiring you now."

Phil was ready to go off on her, but heard a familiar voice behind him say, "Daddy, there is the angel! The one who saved me."

Phil turned around away saw the Pakistani kid. He was holding the hand of the Subway manager who had threatened him less than 24 hours ago.

The man who was now a familiar figure to Phil, gave him a grateful head nod and said, "You...you...you saved my son. You kept your promise to me. You kept your word. You put the hot dog mafia away for good. You are true hero. How can I thank you?"

"Do you have four-grand you could give me? Or a loan and I'll pay back when I write my masterpiece."

"I don't have much money, but I can offer you a job. You can be a manager at my Subway."

"How much?"

"Thirteen bucks, full time."

Missy looked to be calculating the money in her. "Phil. You would be able to pay the court in less than 90 days and have free meals,"

"Yeah, I would, wouldn't I," said Phil. "I could write poems when it got slow. This sounds like a good fucking gig."

The Pakistani man let go of his son's hand, held Phil's and said, "My son believes you are an angel and I do too. No matter what kind of filth comes from your mouth and the wicked words you write, you will have food and honest pay. You are friend and now my employee Philip. Allah Hu Akbar."

"Well, ram a lam a ding dong. Yeah, I fucking love sandwiches and Missy does too," said Phil.

"Very good. It is a deal," the Subway owner said, "May Allah bless you."

"Daddy, aren't angels already blessed by Allah."

The father laughed. He and smiled and rubbed his son's head. "Very true son. Very true. So Mr. LoPresti, you will start Subway management this Monday?"

"Hell yeah, I'll be there."

"Very good," the Subway Manager said and then hugged Phil. "Thank you. Thank so much."

The man let go of Phil and took his son's hand. They walked away leaving Phil alone with Missy.

It was just the two of them in front of the church. Phil noticed Missy was smiling and there was a glow in her eyes. He wanted that smile to always be in his life, during the good and during the inevitable bad times.

He got down on his knee, held Missy's hand, and said, "Missy, let's go get married in that fucking church."

"What?" she said in shock.

"I want to fucking marry you, Missy. Since I burnt off Peter Sotos' face and almost got killed by the mob, I see what I want and that is to marry you."

"Are you serious?" said Missy.

"Yeah, I know that the world is still fucked but it will be less fucked if we got married so I knew you'd always be in my life."

Missy smiled and said, "Stop fucking around, Phil."

"I'm not. I'm really not, Missy. I got a good job now and I've got a good woman, so fuck it. The few good things in life you get you hold to, you hold to them tight. I love you more than anything, so let's go marry each other in that fucking pedo church."

Missy's smile only increased as she took his hand and said, "Ok. Let's get married. I love you, YOU FUCK."

ACKNOWLEDGMENTS

Philip LoPresti is one of my favorite poets and this book is a tribute to him. I worked on this book after my mother passed away and had finished writing *Slasher Camp for Nerd Dorks*. I needed to laugh and get out a lot of angst. This book provided me a place to do that and kept me from the darkness. Thank you Phil, you inspire me as much as the classic TV show *Silk Stalkings*.

ABOUT THE AUTHOR

Christoph Paul is an award-winning humor author. He writes non-fiction, YA, Bizarro, horror, and poetry including: *The Passion of the Christoph, Great White House Volume 1* and *Volume 2*, Slasher Camp for Nerd Dorks, and Horror Film Poems. He is the managing editor for CLASH Media and CLASH Books and edited the anthologies *Walk Hand in Hand Into Extinction: Stories Inspired by True Detective* and *This Book Ain't Nuttin to Fuck With: A Wu-Tang Tribute Anthology.* Under the pen name Mandy De Sandra, he writes Bizarro Erotica that has been covered in VICE, Huffington Post, Jezebel, and AV Club. He is represented by Veronica Park at the Corvisiero Literary Agency.

For More Information

christophpaulauthor.com

christophpaulwriter@gmail.com

ALSO BY CHRISTOPH PAUL

Slasher Camp for Nerd Dorks

Horror Film Poems

Social Media for Anti-Socials: #HowToUseTwitter

Great White House Vol. 1 & Vol. 2

The Passion of the Christoph

Editor

This Book Ain't Nuttin to Fuck With: A Wu-Tang Tribute Anthology

Walk Hand and Hand Into Extinction: Stories Inspired by True Detective

CPSIA information can be obtained
at www.ICGtesting.com
Printed in the USA
FSHW04n2048130418
46969FS